MONSTER KNOWS

EXCUSE ME

by Connie Colwell Miller

illustrated by Maira Chiodi

PICTURE WINDOW BOOKS
a capstone imprint

Monster's shopping with his mom.

There's lots to see and do.

Monster knows his manners

and when to use them too.

JAM

JAM   JAM

4

Mommy needs a cart to shop.
The man here needs one too.
Monster steps aside for him.
"EXCUSE ME. Please pass through."

5

Snoodle
Sneech

Snoodle
Sneech

Snoodle
Sneech

Snoodle
Sneech

Snoodle
Sneech

7

Monster hurries down an aisle
and bumps another cart.

"EXCUSE ME, sir," Monster says,
"for that mistake on my part."

Monster sees a friend nearby.

But Monster doesn't shout.

He waits and says, "EXCUSE ME, friend.
So good to see you out."

Mommy stops to chat a bit.
Monster interrupts the two.

Monster knows his mistake.

CLYDE

EXCUSE ME. I WAS RUDE.

13

Next Monster's shopping happily.

He feels an urge—Uh-oh!

14

"EXCUSE ME, Mom," he says softly.
"I really have to go."

MONSTER
RESTROOM

Now Monster's back and moving on.

There's shopping left to do.

A monster moving quickly
drops her wallet on the floor.

Monster picks it up for her.

EXCUSE ME.
IS THIS YOURS?

19

Monster helps Mom with the food.

The clerk adds up the bill.

"EXCUSE ME, miss," Monster says.

"You forgot this lemon krill."

SBLERG......1.00
BLIPUM......3.50
eGGS........4.10

Now that shopping is all done,
Monster gets a sweet.

READ MORE

Dahl, Michael. *Hippo Says Excuse Me*. Hello Genius. North Mankato, Minn.: Picture Window Books, 2012.

Goldberg, Whoopi. *Whoopi's Big Book of Manners*. New York: Hyperion Books for Children, 2006.

Smith, Sian. *Manners in the Community*. Oh, Behave! Chicago: Heinemann Library, 2013.

INTERNET SITES

FactHound offers a safe, fun way to find Internet sites related to this book. All of the sites on FactHound have been researched by our staff.

Here's all you do:

Visit www.facthound.com

Type in this code: 9781479522026

Super-cool stuff! Check out projects, games and lots more at www.capstonekids.com

Look for all the books in the series:

Thanks to our adviser for his expertise, research, and advice:
Terry Flaherty, PhD, Professor of English
Minnesota State University, Mankato

Editor: Shelly Lyons
Designer: Ashlee Suker
Art Director: Nathan Gassman
Production Specialist: Laura Manthe
The illustrations in this book were created digitally.

Picture Window Books are published by Capstone.
1710 Roe Crest Drive, North Mankato, Minnesota 56003
www.capstonepub.com

Library of Congress Cataloging-in-Publication Data
Cataloging-in-publication information is on file with the Library of Congress.
978-1-4795-2202-6 (library binding)
978-1-4795-2965-0 (board book)
978-1-4795-2953-7 (paperback)
978-1-4795-3328-2 (eBook pdf)
Written by Connie Colwell Miller

Printed in the United States of America in North Mankato, Minnesota.
092013   007772CGS14